ALL SAIL NO RUDDER

Printed in the United States of America

Whitehead, Frederick E.

All Sail No Rudder/Whitehead- 1st Edition

ISBN: 978-0-9896220-7-3

1. All Sail No Rudder – Poetry 2. New Author – No Frills Buffalo. 3. Poetry.
1. Title

Cover art by Joseph R. Thiel- jrthiel.com
Author photograph by Michael Want

No Frills Buffalo Press
119 Dorchester
Buffalo, New York 14213
For more information visit
Nofrillsbuffalo.com

ALL SAIL NO RUDDER

By Frederick E. Whitehead

it is,
every bit of it,
revision.

This one is for my parents.

Introduction by David Landrey

Reading *All Sail, No Rudder*, I feel as Hawthorne must have felt reading *Moby-Dick*;

"...eternity spread before him and the mysteries of life played out against its backdrop."

Fred Whitehead's poems approach eternity again and again, seeking access, expressing wonderment at how our minds and spirits try to reach it, try and fail and try again. So many attempts, so many failures; yet the efforts are never in vain. Consider "the heron": rising in the dusk "as if she knew/exactly where the portal is"

Ah, that portal: always at the brink of the poet's language and found in such diverse entities as birds, cats, a crab, memories, dreams. Whitehead is led to his language and through these things by a hovering muse, a "he/she", whose influence at once highlights the elusiveness of language and brings him to its brink:

> as she painted
> the trip
> this way of hers
>
> I could only think
> of myself
> little more
> than a boneyard
> where beautiful phrases
> go to die.

There are many "trips" in *All Sail, No Rudder*. There is the voyage, through generations, beginning when the poet is "learning/to master language" as he watches an elder die; visits to Florida and elsewhere; and – magically - the stream of our lives as captured in "water":

> I've heard it said
> that all of the water
> in the world today
> is the very same
> that has ever been.

Recognizing throughout his links to all of time, Whitehead has, "crawled through cold/alleys of the city listening for clues"; and oh, he finds them, even though "the words escape me," "leaving me with no way/to colorfully describe/... my collapsing universe." He finds the clues again and again, even-perhaps especially- in "the core of January," finding the

> inner fire to
> melt any fears
> that threaten to freeze
> out the dreams
> that keep one
> forging ahead

So read on and see Fred Whitehead "retrieve my/scattered children/the parts of me/now gone," and celebrate the miracle that "I/had once again/survived the cull" as he follows the "lamp of morning" held by his muse.

- August 2013
Mr. Landrey is a retired professor from Buffalo State College and the author of *Consciousness Suite*

watching her read Wanting To Die

the year I was learning
to master language
she was in her living

room reading
Wanting To Die

I watch her now the only way
I can, in
shades of gunmetal and dust

film of her in a chair
breathing her intention
the light

fighting to escape eyes
that catch the lens
on all the right syllables

postman

the flag snaps
in the breeze that seems
to sidestep neighborhood holdouts,
whose lungs
match that of
the sidewalk's wheeze
back alleys
belch fetid warning
trash barrels roll along the gutter
bankorphaned proprietors don't
shelvestock
anything sustaining to life
beer cigarettes lottery stubs,
the empty remains of which
hold masses of gratitude
for the addicted, they
multiply along the rotting
clapboard storefronts
with plastic tubes
of frozen sugar water
their colors gone
sucked dry by
shoeless children who
run in happy packs
as long as light remains
the congregants of the old church
repeat tracts of their youth
to the congregants of the new
but the choir isn't singing
the pipes have gone silent
and the bells
only ring at noon
signifying some divide in the day
sending little more into

the air than flocks
of pigeons
their flight tracked daily
by the postman
who may have had words
of significance for all of this
stored in the flask of forgetfulness
he holds as holy in his hip pocket
its weight offsetting
the weight which he carries
but the words, if he had them
would only be lost
among the unopened envelopes
and their meaning beaten into
shell shocked dogs
by the desperate and forgotten

what Gregor knew

we are
confined by the laws of
inheritance

documenting the results
of dominant and recessive traits
for ourselves
trying to decipher
coded trajectory
we
sway like pods
in an abbey garden
waiting to be
harvested
and opened
for observation

vertical evacuation

scanning the horizon
gifted to me
watching for sunrise
waiting with the rest

all of us
doing what's expected
of ourselves

all the while listening
for that little chime
announcing the start
of our
vertical evacuation

water

I've heard it said
that all of the water
in the world today
is the very same
that has ever been

so the tear I shed at your departing
this morning may have, at one time,
been one that fell from
Hagar's eye at her expulsion

or perhaps it was a long ago trickle of
snow melt in the Pyrenees
or part of a much smaller Colorado
as it was just getting down to
the business of carving out canyons

part of the flood waters that
devastated New Orleans
or, I suppose, dew settling
on the canopy of a virgin
rain forest

and for that matter, feeling as I did
as your stockinged legs disappeared into the
cab, it may very well have, at one time,

been the piss of
some Homo Erectus chap
hissing on the remains
of a fire
somewhere on a vast plain

long before we ever
invented words
for explaining things
such as this

imagining what was in his head
while walking by his door

my adrenaline well
had dried up
about the time I lost hope
of waltzing out of
the armed doors
to be among the
creatures so wonderfully rendered
in marble and scattered about
the landscaped perfection
of the grounds

even my occasional hobby
of measuring
my degree of decrepitude
against that of the other residents
holds little interest
for me anymore

so I wait
with tenacious grasp
on the tether
for the man in the
starched smock to
pronounce
soul blind
that the lives of my
children are now officially
post-burden

but, levitation,
now that is another matter
at times, when all I can hear is
a room alarm blaring unanswered

in another part of the building
I float out of this bed
take my fishing gear down from
the garage wall
to stand knee deep
in a creek
my wife not ten yards away
young again
in her straw hat
and fashionable sun glasses
reading the book
she was
reading the month
she went on ahead
her small hand
going to her lips
to retrieve and release
the last kiss
reserved for us

retrieve

I may have known
without knowing
the doubt that lay
within it
I may have carved it
in marvelous
callous sun
I may have heard it
bouquet of bourbon
brethren singing
with lungs
of perestroika
of railroad strike
enslavement
faulty tenor
riding terror
in ancient
mother tongue
I may have danced
without shoe
or sacred bending
let the earth
rise to meet me
lizard regenerating bone
I may have seen
seasons of forgiveness
seas of transmutation
seeking information
in this and all of this
if told that I've been done
by someone
complete
I could conceive it
I could believe in sheltered

evenings
I could retrieve my
scattered children
the parts of me
now gone

such is breakfast with a Buddhist poet

often, when I'm
alone, my pen
holding back in
indignation, I have
a vision

in which
I am at a table
with Milarepa
who isn't paying
attention to anything
I have to say about
world affairs or
the point spread of
the Bowl game
or the latest offering
from Detroit, in fact

he doesn't even acknowledge
the waitress
as she
hovers the bottomless
coffee pot over our table,
the geriatric choking
on his home fries
in the booth beside us
or even my request for him
to hand me the pepper sauce

he just sits across from me
a strangely blissful look
on his face
as my eggs get cold
and go unseasoned

his right hand
cupped to his ear
listening,
always
listening
to
the sound
of emptiness

this mirror so deserving of anger

this mirror so
deserving of anger
has in it's heart
a vision of Hades
so stand
in it's fire
and rage on
a mad
servant
to it's dire sting

blue cat by back steps

a stay
a cable
a kept pet
blue cat
by back steps
paces
pace paced

the night I was a jackass to
a blue crab in Delmarva

childlike meanness
I suppose
was all it was
that and the fact that
I was a six pack into
a warm night
on the beach
and, I must add,
he did kind of
sneak up on me
so, I let a stream of
tobacco juice fly

a perfect shot,   yeah boy

right between the eye stalks
I thought that
would send
him scurrying
but he just backed away

slowly

one claw clicking
crustacean code
for a few universally
common words
the meaning
of which
I know
all too well

the professor

"it's about all you can do, really"
that's usually
how the night's talks
begin

most times, it's how
they end too

I took the beer he offered,
nodded a thanks
and settled in to drink it slowly
and to listen
even slower

he went on
about squaring his deal
with whatever deities are
at the helm of this sinking
tub we huddle in,
coloring his phrasing
as only an artist can -
forty second songs
about dreams falling
away like petals in autumn

psalms about mortgages
and medical bills, woven in
scales and harmonies
in such a way
that they stick with you
for days

he poured a glass with a
perfect head and stared into it
as if the voice of
an oracle that only
he could hear
relayed messages
from long dead sages
from somewhere within
that ambered vessel

"I heard once" he said
"I don't remember where,
but it went something like,
like, if you try to live your
grandparents' religion
your are basically committing
spiritual plagiarism"
"I like that" I said
"yea" he said "me too"

then, I could see another shift
coming
his eyes foreshadowing
a turn in the conversation
so I slid a fresh coaster
out of the rack,
waited for him to finish
tapping a pint
and prepared
myself
for another
long night
of learning

the core of January

with the clearing of
the path
finished,
I lean the shovel against
the side of the shed
and stand for
a minute in
wind relentless
and flesh out a memory

trying to rework it
into a vision,
one warm enough
to melt the snow
around my boots
and the snow
on my shoulders
and the small ice dams
around my eyes

I strain to see through
frost that always seems
at its heaviest around
the core of January
when certain frigid
realizations float like
bergs on the surface
of short hard days

when
I have no control over
the shakes, when
I can't seem to get my hands
to move in

logical patterns
and thoughts of endless winter
occupy a sizable amount time

but there is a load of wood
cradled in my aching arms
as I head for
a door that really
is closer than
it seems
and somewhere
there is a part of my history
moving through this world

hopefully in comfort
hopefully full in a life
hopefully quiet of mind
and steady of heart
and I pray
in possession of an
inner fire to
melt any fears
that threaten to freeze
out the dreams
that keep one
forging ahead

listening to animals

at first I thought
I was alone but
they were all there
reciting the liturgy of the universe
each in
particular vernacular
telling me that,
when I am done
I will float away
and that I will
no longer have to haul
around the weight of
my mistakes
or worry about
living up to the
archetype of some hero
shaped by some great epic
and I don't know how
it was that I understood
all of this babbling
coming from
tree and brush but
I knew what they meant
when they told me that
I would no longer be
afraid of eclipsed suns,
things in
the corners of
unfamiliar rooms
or the unreliable
elasticity of time

sparrow hawking

above the metered
terraced steps
where I
conduct my malady
the arc of the kestrel
from arm to quarry
is art without effort -
wing beat staccato
a soprano's cry

her country drive

when she came back
from her afternoon drive
in the country
I had no choice but to
put my pen away
and turn my uninspired
pages face
down on the desk

and when she said
that she had the
kind of
day that opened
up before her
as the land,
away from the city,
had done,
I could do nothing but
lean against the
kitchen counter,
watch her arrange some
flowers she picked up
at a roadside stand and
listen as she described
how it was so bright
so clear

she said,
the sky was
the color of apricots
early, and later
the color of
Sinatra's eyes
and the air,

she sang,
smelled
like baby clothes

as she painted
the trip in
this way of hers

I could only think
of myself as
little more
than a boneyard
where beautiful phrases
go to die

he knows only the rain

July blinked awake,
a retiree coming out
of a nap,
rising to the low end
bellow of a bullfrog
singing to the cycle

evoking the ancestors
to explain
what it was
that moved him
in this controlled forward fall

what of the zodiacal
display of fireflies
above his boggy territory

and what it was
about the rain that
always made him take to
the road with others
like himself -
dodging rolling beasts
in the downpour

leaving the young behind
to lose their tails
and break the surface
he may well hear their
chorus of longing the
next time the sky
resets its signs

but for now
he knows only the rain
and how
it keeps him moving

digging in the trench of memory

the night came on one minute
and twenty seconds earlier
tonight than it did yesterday

alone, I ladled out a fair amount
of disillusion gumbo
readied the spoon, steadied
my resolve and dug in

digging in the trench
of memory
one spoonful at a time
chewing long on the wrong turns
and the amount of time
spent pushing the string

now that the light has turned
to velvet outside
the window
the meal done
I dabbed the corners
of my downturned mouth
and push away from the table

there's a page waiting
to be filled in
and a pen waiting
to be emptied

and sleep
tapping on my forehead
demanding I
pay the vig on my loan

fly

what good
are these wings
if we are allowed only
to circle your crowned head
leashed by
a single strand
of your
starlight
hair

apologies to a violet

the cat just blinks
at my question
"now, when did this die?"

she lowers her head to her paws
as I bring the remains
in close for visual autopsy

it feels lighter now
as if something has
departed other
than just the water
that held its soil
in order

I remember watering it
just the other day
however, my
just the other days
are just as easily
just last week
last month...
the distant past

how many more victims
of my sporadic care
will go the way of
this once vibrant violet?

that's the thing with attentiveness

you have to pay attention

another measure of focus
that never fails to elude me

still, as I was hoping
for some kind of
vegetable based Lazarus
I water it -
too much so

leaving the cat
to lap at the pool that
spreads out
around the ceramic pot

like a mourner
helping herself to a cup of tea
at a funeral breakfast

knots

if I were to
go blind, I could still
trace these senses back
along a knotted silver thread
I would
feel the years
between my forefinger
and thumb
until I came
to the largest one
I would pinch
it until it left
indelible, an
impression,
a vermillion mark
for a particular August
then work my way
forward again
counting knots
of all the milestones
you were not here

witness

wait for lapis
blue drawn curtain
take the
hand that needs
to be
whispers drip lilacs
tip
to the cheek a greeting
luminous
newborn eye
of indigo night
witness to
sacred union
this

the lamp of morning

when I saw you
holding the crystal up
to the column of dawn
                    I wondered
what it was you saw because
as I readied myself
for another day
of mystery
not knowing
what I'd have to face
you were so sure about yours
the orb in your hand
multiplying the light
in spiral waves
that seemed to cleanse
the air of worry
I looked up as I said
goodbye from the hall
                         - it was a moment,
as you turned and smiled,
that held before me
the lamp of morning

pyramid

I never saw you through
the tormented years
of your youth
as you never
saw me through mine
and yet
we navigate around
them still
a perfect invisible
pyramid of dead rats
and horse shit
in the middle of
whatever room we are in
its apex pointing
the way to Drago
the method of its
construction
a mystery
and its dimensions
a mathematical twin
to the combined
length and breadth
of all
we have become

the words escape me

when I am lost in a commercial
for a product guaranteed
to rid my lungs
of that damned incorrigible mucus,
this is what they do

as I stare at the screen
the words are filing
through the bars of
their gray cells

I may be whistling
 a bit of Carmen
while tracing the contours of
ceramic animal life
in layered dust on their
book shelf abode
as the words
are creeping along an outer wall
hidden by tall grass and
hoping for a fault in the stonework

later, of course,
I will
look for them
but by then
they will have long ago
shimmied up a tree by the
edge of the enclosure
and have made that great
leap for freedom

still, I will go on
a lantern held before me,
a pencil behind an ear
a notebook in the back
pocket of my jeans
knowing that, once again
they are gone

leaving me with no way
to colorfully describe
the thought processes of librarians,
my neighbor's garden,
the shopkeeper's lack of social skills
or, seemingly,
my collapsing universe

the throne of memory

catatonic decommissioned fogbound
returned
to a home
nonexistent except
on tattered maps
and in conversations of
those who kept
pre-deployed history
alive with abridged laughter
photos some
familiar music
seldom heard names
details of
their recent lives
no eye
could have seen the way
he moved inside or
how his addictions to
cognac corpses cordite
made him
an oak waiting for the axe
to rape its way through
the rough shell
and when
finally exposed
the heartwood
shrank and cracked
under the heat
of judgment
and as expected
ashes took their
rightful place
on the throne
of memory

meerschaum

she tamped
the words into
her journal
a laid back manner
of compacting sentences
short fragrant
phrases
worked in with
relaxed hand
then it is
set
aside
a pipe,
filled and waiting
for the world
to strike
the match

the speed in which he left

one day before he turned one
hundred he died, that was back in nineteen and
eighty, now what's left of him is
six feet below the surface of Pittsburgh, a
thousand people there, come from
miles around to see him off, he lived a day and a half
per day his whole life, and wasn't about to give one
second more, no sir, not a one

ancient and unusual

if I become both
of these
not just one or the other
but both, together
at the end of this run,
then I will finally
have the shroud
of accomplishment
I have always hoped for
with it I will
cover up
as I slip between
dimensions to
sleep off the effects
of one life
and prepare myself
for another

try

celebrating the small
miracle that I
had once again
survived the cull

another day
ducking the net,
skipping over the bolas

able to drop my keys
on the table
by the door I use
to shut myself away

oh how
psychosis wants the mind
cirrhosis the liver
family your attention
employer your time

but, I've made it through again
entering
these mortgaged rooms
with their faded scent
of seasons past

over the hum of the
refrigerator's tired compressor
and the dripping
of an un-serviced faucet
I hear her laughter upstairs

which reminds me yet again
to try to
do that myself
a little more often

proving a love

I'm not sure
how it could be explained
to the authorities,
besides that,
there are easier ways
to prove my existence
other than
digging up and reassembling
my bones

just remembering
our conversations should
do it, I mean

we spent a fair amount
of adolescent evenings
sitting with
stolen beer on the
steps behind the school

all of that talking

hours spent on the seasons,
on constellations,
our belief in or lack of a god,
your dreams of Europe
and mine of mountain seclusion

you made it to Europe
and I waited,
just laid down
and waited

and I was real

you knew that then,
you do now,
at least a part
of you does

the part of you
that isn't throwing dirt
over a shoulder
one shovelful at
a time

palette

every morning
I re-paint your portrait

pigments of earth
shades of memory

no brush -
just fingers dipped in
colors of absentia

dabbed on canvas
of separating years
and left to fade
until another daybreak

calls me to
the palette again

good

today, at least,
you were still there
- where my arms end

a good thing, that.

good measured in
quiet welcome -
measured in
study of face,
intent
of eye

naturally

stepping out of the
air conditioned room
to look to the quadrant

of the Florida sky that
I heard the
local meteorologist say
would be holding Mars

I couldn't fight the thoughts of
pulling a Houdini
and staying beachside forever

every night from here on in
would be spent
with you sleeping on fresh linen
and me with my sand covered feet

on the railing of a balcony
drawing slowly from a cold beer
and squinting upward

waiting for the God of war
to make an appearance

arrival

once while
waiting for the meteor's
appearance during
a forecast shower of such

I wondered what their
cries must be like
as they break from
the silence of space

into the unready arms
of Mother Earth

today I sat in a plastic chair

today
I sat in a plastic chair
on the patio
messing around with a
guitar I hadn't played in a while

just a few chords
here and there between
sips of iced tea
clumsily picking runs
through scales I somehow
managed to remember

the cats were
in the window over
my shoulder, watching birds
and sniffing the June air
listening to me hack away
on a lazy afternoon

with their eyes closed
I suppose they thought
themselves cougars
lounging on branches of
forest trees
waiting for prey

and when I closed mine
I was Rodrigo
giving life to
a masterpiece for the world

I played as
hills rose all around me
the wind blowing off of Erie
became a
Mediterranean breeze

that carried
my Concierto
through the village
up to the ruins of the
citadel, for Roman
ghosts to weep over

he sits

he sits at the kitchen table
and talks about the dead
as if they had just passed
him the cream and took from
him the sugar

in a white t-shirt
pushing around
a jumble of mail
and newspapers
he talks about the dead
as if they just finished
their coffee and adjusted
their greasy ball caps

he sits
in this compressed time -
the years slipped
into the small pocket
on the bib of his overalls

and talks about the dead
as if they just rose
from the chairs around him
and tapped him on the shoulder
as they walked by him and
out of the front door
into morning

on a branch of a magnolia tree above the mound

in some eclectic approach to
the song of mourning
the dove cooed in
counter time
with the cricket

sawing out the rhythm
of a missing heart's beat
somewhere in the grass

there
where the headstone will go

a sense of absence

is all
that is
left in your palm
while trying not to miss a moment
feel what it is to be krill
thrashing in
the baleen of the universe

too anxious
to open a locked box
two o'clock unpopulated
afternoon walk
past picket fences
pockets rattle with last night's broken charms
this
is the yoke fitted to
your specifications
the gift of intuition lifted with
not a twist of difference
the jinn's influence
takes hold one
whisper at a time

polemic piranhas taking
what they will from your stand
always
of course
always
with patience

the numbers lean toward
becoming nothing more
than just another cretin
lurking at the at edge of the parade

elbowing aside
the unsuspecting weak
to catch trinkets thrown from floats
sadly wired to waiting
for your name to be carried
on the unified voice of the marchers
never knowing when to turn away

the place

you arrive alone and
in between the getting there
and escaping the
place you escaped to
in the first place
peace did not
descend from
the heavens

outside
the sidewalks offer up
familiar emotionless faces
bobbing on top of
the same bloated corpses
that always float by
propelled by dark energy and
restlessness

inside
clean ones in clean suits
try to out brag each other
over their manhattans or
mohitos or whatever the hell

waitresses hide their
disdain for these assholes
behind skewed smiles,
your team just lost in overtime,
and the Midwest has conspired
to send a cold front
right down the very street
you are fated to
walk every night

but it's o.k.
because you've been blessed
with the gift of not caring
which is as close to nirvana
as you are
ever going to get

St. Augustine

we were there once
I tried to find
history playback
in the eyes of the lions

I wondered about the
outpost as she led
me by my elbow
toward the
old city

with its brass placards
its cobbled roads
its foreign made trinkets

next to the schoolhouse,
or courthouse,
I leaned on
the bleached planking,
souvenir shirts draped
over an arm,
watched domesticated
seabirds filching
scraps from cans
awaiting

her return
with necklaces adorned
with shells and sea turtles
and sand dollars

she asked my opinion
as I held them up
I answered with approval

as I imagined the lions would
with little sound,
a gentle nuzzle

I pawed them
into the white paper bag
with its blue lettering
and leaping dolphin
as she pointed at
some other bright thing
ahead of us
saying
that we should come
back again
someday

the heron

the heron
over Ontario
her silhouette,
prehistoric in the dusklight,
rising from this,
the last lake in the chain

I watched until
the coming night
swallowed her
somewhere
out there
over the water
as if she knew
exactly where the portal is

from the darkness I see

the shadows
taking up positions as
wind, time and sea
work at bringing down
the cliffs - they wait as
continents are
turned into pebbles
pebbles
into sand

the shadows
roam my hallways
adjusting portraits and
rearranging items
on tables as
they work light switches

bulbs don't ignite,
from the darkness I see
authority testing the weak
nature rolling over
children reclassified
illnesses being invented

the soft hand
of grace goes
into a pocket
and stays there

Calliope sneered

you know, there was a day when I
held close the notion
that all of those
tales of possibility were true

it is so I have my ways and I,
dosed on potion,
have crawled through cold
alleys of the city listening for clues

don't I now hear baying and cries?
for those chosen
to fall will know
failing and atrocities, the ruse

repeated again
then again
until even nostalgia,
unable to win
the battle of memory and truth,

will curl into itself and keep
the mysterious history of sleep
safe from
the hands of the muse

flower empress

in the garden
she stands
as if preparing a
grand emergence from
inherited dreamscape
attired in astral illusion
azalea has bloomed
as iris awaits
I concern myself with
protocol
enter to be her escort out,
or wait
as she synchronizes her appearance
with the cycle of songbirds
she holds the attention
of the crocus and I
buckets of rain
arm dead
and the day
ready
to move along

memories of church

his diatribe on morality
and miracle was
going into the third quarter
and I started to wonder
if I was up to the
challenge of
sustained attention

dragged in and chained to
a pew by believing,
well intentioned parents
I languished as tradition
shifted on the hard benches
and coughed up dust
in the echoey chamber -

for me,
it was in the throes of death

I hummed its requiem
while the seconds
stretched before me,
an unending chain of
rat turds leading
to fetid nests constructed
within the heart of man

there were things I needed
to get done
there were
bodies to be pulled from
a river of contemplation
and stacked along
it's twisted banks

for carrion to consider

I had a universe
to paint on the vaulted ceiling
of my summer days,
trails to blaze,
girls to impress

I fought exhaustion as stained
morning light fell upon
the lamb of my parents,
my eyes went to the exit
as the call to hymn
had me doubting
identity
and validity of
the word

a simple wish

as I rise,
my wish: simply
to be allowed to move,
mostly unhindered

a mid-range note
listening for its echo
in the
improvisation
of the day

among the wreckage

like Simonides
identifying the dead
I pinpoint positions
in the rubble
where all of
my intentions
had gathered -
to hear the victory ode
and raise their wine
to a world collapsing
around them

waiting on the solstice

then there was the time
the guy in charge
misplaced the key
to unlock the solstice

summer was delayed
so we
stood around
looking to the east

shuffling in the dirt
making small talk
about transition

do (a suggestion)

fixate on the present
rotate on your heels
contemplate catastrophe
frustrate peers
irritate neighbors
eliminate yesterday
inflate balloons
deflate egos
narrate your life to anyone
who will listen
expatriate from yourself
regurgitate from lecterns
plait your locks
propagate purpose
hate ignorance
state facts as you perceive them
initiate change
dictate your history
rate higher
regulate criticism
gyrate for no particular reason
relate to nature
instigate peace
sedate demons
delegate during disruption
bait those in power
eradicate inherited viruses
radiate aural significance
infiltrate inner spaces
create conscious authority
eliminate darkness
dilate your eyes in the
sun of your days

climb

another morning
spent

under
exhaustive questions
by a high priced Sherpa

commissioned to
guide her
to some emotional summit
she was
convinced
she

• had to conquer

instructed to unload
all she had packed for the ascent

feeling
none the lighter
for any of it

rose

she had grown tired
of being the rose -
wishing to initiate
instant change
and limp away from
her role as
the jewel of the garden
the chance to
sit on the porch
and interject her own
inconsistencies to familiar stories
would never come
she knew she would not
be allowed to lay low
when storms came
nor to dance
when they passed
she could only carry on
as the lilies bowed in reverence
and the sun flowers towered
above her

sides

there is no wall
between sanity
and insanity
just a rope line
velvet
with a silver hook
and a bouncer
who is known to
take bribes

counting the cross ties

if I am found
some morning
beside the track
let them know that I
ran out of numbers

it was
nothing more
than that

war fever

she could do nothing
to cure the culture
that infected
the man engaging his country's enemy
in his old room
in the home

of the woman holding
a cold rag
to his forehead

hush now, honey
we got
to bring
this war fever down
she said

she opened the window
to let January blow across
his dessert
and sat as he crushed
her hand,
waiting for recognition
to return to his eyes

she prayed the same unanswered
prayer,
she cursed the same unaccountable
men

she stayed until he shuddered
to sleep at dawn
then she left, with a

a light on and the window open
just in case his spirit
was still searching
for the way home

momentary transport

the coffee,
or most of it anyway,
stayed in the cup as I
made my groggy walk
to the beach
the mornings here,
devoid of
other vacationers,
is cleansing
if I may employ a term my wife
uses to
describe ridding one's self
of all the crap we tend
to collect
I try to remember where
Nantucket is from the
map on the cottage wall
and raise the souvenir cup
so that its
schooner is
on the correct heading
gifting myself
momentary transport
before turning back
in the direction
of breakfast

boxed doves

a basket of sand dollars
of different sizes
and prices was
placed strategically near
the register

an easy grab for
someone looking
for a simple buy for
somebody back home

I first learned of
this fragile marine currency
from the lady in the corner house
on the street where
I grew up

she gave me a few
which I kept in a cigar box
some intact
some broken with purpose
to set free the doves within
though their migratory route
was like that
of so many of us

covering only the distance
from one end of
a box to the other

tiki

they have,
since the time
of their
Polynesian birth,
spread to taverns
anywhere oceans
kiss the land

even here
in old New England
Kane is pouring
Kanaloa drinking

it wouldn't be surprising at all
to see them watching over
a crowded bar in Omsk,
where palm fronds
and ushankas mix
in a pineapple and rum haze

over time
they have been smuggled
inward to infiltrate
landlocked bars

so that the likes of Austin and
Edmonton, Berlin and Bucharest
can partake equally
in the nectar
of tiki gods

three blues

1:
a soft contingent of
slate hued yesterdays curled
up inside my chest

2:
they just don't build blue
like this anymore
so I do believe I'll
hang on to
it for a bit longer

3:
it was this morning
when despair wiped
his feet on the mat
took off his hat and
nodded a cordial nod
I remembered that familiar smile
and tell me,
has an eye ever
reflected the slow blue
pulse of sorrow
like that
I don't think one ever has

Acknowledgments

The author would to thank the reader for making it all the way through the book, unless of course the reader starts the book from the back (as the author has been wont to do). In either case the author thanks the reader and hopes you enjoyed or will enjoy the poems, as the case may be.

Much love to Tammy for her unending support.

A special thanks to David Landrey for his assistance in editing this volume.

And last, to Life, for the material.

www.ingramcontent.com/pod-product-compliance
Lightning Source LLC
LaVergne TN
LVHW010939110826
845149LV00013B/2680
* 9 7 8 0 9 8 9 6 2 2 0 7 3 *